TO:

_____

FROM:

_____

DATE:

_____

Do not fear, for I am with you;

do not be afraid, for I am your God.

I will strengthen you; I will help you;

I will hold on to you with my righteous right hand.

~Isaiah 41:10~

Be strong and courageous; don't
be terrified or afraid of them.
For the LORD your God is the
one who will go with you; he will
not leave your or abandon you.
~Deuteronomy 31:6~

Therefore we do not
give up. Even though our
outer person is
being destroyed, our
inner person is being
renewed day by day.
~2 Corinthians 4:16–18~

Trust in the LORD with all
your heart, and do not rely on
your own understanding.
~Proverbs 3:5~

Because of the LORD's
faithful love we do not
perish, for his mercies
never end. They are new
every morning; great is
your faithfulness!
~Lamentations 3:22–23~

Do nothing out of selfish
ambition or conceit,
but in humility consider
others as more important
than yourselves.
~Philippians 2:3~

Let us run with
endurance the race
that lies before us,
keeping our eyes on
Jesus, the source and
perfecter of our faith.
~Hebrews 12:1–2~

> The one who walks with the
> wise will become
> wise, but a companion of
> fools will suffer harm.
> ~Proverbs 13:20~

"The LORD your God is among you, a warrior who saves. He will rejoice over you with gladness. He will be quiet in his love. He will delight in you with singing.
~Zephaniah 3:17~

Trust in the LORD forever,
because in the LORD, the LORD
himself, is an everlasting rock!
~Isaiah 26:4~

The Lord does not delay his promise, as some understand delay, but is patient with you, not wanting any to perish but all to come to repentance.
~2 Peter 3:9~

> Blessed is the one who
> endures trials, because when he
> has stood the test he will receive
> the crown of life that God has
> promised to those who love him.
> ~James 1:12~

Do not be conformed
to this age, but be
transformed by the
renewing of your mind,
so that you may discern
what is the good,
pleasing, and perfect
will of God.
~Romans 12:2~